Seedlip and Sweet Apple

Seedlip and Sweet Apple

Arra Lynn Ross

Published 2010 by Milkweed Editions
Cover design by Cathy Spengler
Cover art, "Woman Waiting, No. 22," by Susan Harbage Page
Interior design by Connie Kuhnz, BookMobile
The text of this book is set in Trajanus
19 20 21 22 23 5 4 3 2
First Edition

Please turn to the back of this book for a list of the sustaining funders of Milkweed
Editions.

Library of Congress Cataloging-in-Publication Data
Ross, Arra Lynn, 1977–
    Seedlip and sweet apple / Arra Lynn Ross. — 1st ed.
      p.   cm.
    Poems
    ISBN 978-1-57131-434-5 (pbk. : alk. paper)
    I. Title.
    PS3618.O84524S44 2010
    811'.6—dc22

                        2009046688

for Ann Lee

Seedlip and Sweet Apple

THE WORD OF LIFE

THE NEW WORLD

JOURNEY OF THE WORD

Seedlip and Sweet Apple

THE WORD OF LIFE

I was once as you are . . .
–Mother Ann

Inside My Skin

1742, Baptism at Christ Church, Manchester, England

In the name of the Father

The words flew up.
The seams of my body   came undone—
my breath—the flutter of a dove's wings,
its shadow bruising the scarlet sun of the altar window,
bruising the golden wheat beetling from its stalk, bruising   the bound sheaves,
the bent head of Jesus on his dark cross.
Tears of warm blood streak his cheeks,
gush into the furrows of his quivering ribs.

and of the Son

Then the bird was gone,   the shadow
of the bird, its opal-throated song—   gone.
I fell back inside
my skin, my seams, my chafing frock, my father's arms.
The tip of a nose, chapped bottom lip, my tongue.
I tasted the water—bittersweet, tasted   a word,
two words, three words, a name, a rose,   a seed,
a longing and an answer, clear and true
as green shoots in the spring.
And as wordless: a sound only, a taste, a touch, a scent

                                                        opening—

and of the Holy

Ecstatic

When we were younger and my brother William still a head below me,
we would run to the pastures and chase sheep,

belting out the loud *baa* as we flew after them,
hands outstretched and waving like scared birds.

As we ran, we turned from each other
till we stood at far sides of the field,

the dirty-wooled sheep between us;
he was a dark body jumping up and down in the mist,

his palms small dots tossing in the air.

Early Work

1745, Manchester, England

I walk home when night is folded tight like a prayer,
wrapped in the woolen overcoat William wore before his arms got too long,
wishing I knew the names of trees;

that tall one at Sorrow and Toad roofs the roads, veils the stars.
The sky is bright tonight, and I can see the dirt clear,
the rutted grooves torn open.

My hands, stiff from winding the warps,
clench up when I sleep and some mornings
I have to pry them apart by knocking one against the other.

I press my fingers backward for about a minute
so they won't curl back down.
Then I straighten the other.

William Tells of a Public Whipping

I worm us through to the front of the crowd. A man killed a fat hare on Blackmoor's land. We'd seen him singing for shillings in the streets, light of bone and laughter, a girl-child on his shoulders, and she with no shoes. Now, he pulls off his waistcoat and stained undershirt, drops his rough flapped hat to the cobblestones, and turns his naked back to take the leather. The baker's wife beside us whistles high and higher till the note breaks, while her boy, barely able to hold his own weight, drops rocks. The sound is lost in the crowd. No one will pay for him, for the hare. The whip slices, again, again, and screams tear the air ragged. His girl scratches at the eyes of the old woman who holds her at the well. Ann grabs my hand and will not let go.

Mother's Touch

Mother squats and stares,
her face wrinkling into frown.
What do you mean, you don't want a marriage?

I'm scared of the hunger.

I dreamt it,

the dark hole eating

the world.

She leans over me, hand sticky with dough,
squeezes my forearm hard, hisses,
don't say no more.

But it's wrong, Momma,
how people touch—
blind flies
feeling for food
and all the meat's rotten.
Wraps me at night,
I can't breathe
it's so tight and wet
like my own skin falling in.
I can taste the sin.

Girl? She's kneeling now,
her eyelids thick with grief.

(My screams wake her
at night.)

We'll find someone nice.
Your father's man, Abraham, has good hands.

Her fingers bruise my lips,
holding back the moans

  but the trembling takes me
  as it always does, deep
  as the crack
  that divides my sleep, night
  after night.
  The sounds steal out
  from somewhere
  darker than me.
  I won't. I can't! I scream,
  striking her face,
  wishing

I could fold the world over
and make it rise up right.

Found

1758, Manchester, England

Sunday morning, Christ Church, mother smoothing the faded blue of her
one good skirt. Nancy and Mary, the two youngest, on either side of me,
heads on my lap, sleeping, dirt-blond curls catching thin brown strands.
My legs ache and I want to stretch them but not wake the girls, and the
preacher's voice drones and rises, thinned like the thread of a forgotten
song. We, the poor, sit in the back pews, sometimes even stand for the full
two hours. My mother is a pious woman, brushes our hair Sundays (all
five boys and three girls) and ties it up with ribbon she keeps in her good
wood box. Made us scrub down the night before: knees jammed high in the
washbasin, scouring backs and necks on the young ones till they're red and
raw, shivering more from the rough touch than cold. I remember her tearing
tangles from my hair, scratching my scalp as if she could gouge out sin. I'm
old for such attention now—wash in the back room, away from William and
George, though he's only ten. I'm staring up at the window, the stained glass
rising high and curved, pointed toward the vaulted ceiling, huge oak beams
rounding the air like rib cages.

I wonder if the word of God gets stuck in the tight joints. The red and
yellow glass glows with low morning sun; a bright heart wreathed in thorns
drips tears of blood on Jesus's dirty feet, and his blue eyes leak water over
the blood. He stretches his hand toward me and in his mouth I see the sun.
It pulses like blood in my own lips, beats a silent tongue against mouth
bones, bearing a language of taps and clicks that I echo with my hand on
my thigh. Mary shifts, opens her eyes and glares at my moving hand, butts
her head against my leg. I move the staccato song to my belly, fingers run-
ning ribbons of rhythm over my flesh. Faster and faster, then one slow, even
beat, another valley of rushes and sudden gaps, the long void and leap of

galloping hands. I fly into Jesus's open mouth, am swallowed, broken into blood beating through veiny loops. His hands move over dead flesh, quivering with new life; I am there, too, in the dark cave, wet dripping on cold hands. I am in his calloused feet, walking uphill through thick clouds of red sand. Words swim from our mouth, thwacking hard tails against teeth; they fall at our feet, and the poor, with bent heads and dry hands, gather them in woven baskets. The baskets unwind, sink roots to earth, shiver leaves in heavy wind, and fall. The people fasten the fallen cross to the empty sky with our body, hammering it together with square nails. A foreign, final cry worms from Jesus's throat: *My Father, why hast thou forsaken me?* And I am silent, waiting in his cooling belly.

Cold water hits my face. I shiver and blink, look up at my mother holding the bucket with one hand, the other on her hip, face red and shaking back and forth. A group has gathered around her, with two feet of space around me, sitting in the dirt, legs splayed. My thighs feel like sacks of coal when I drag them toward my chest and wrap my arms around them. Fingers thick like grubs, breasts like iron. My head thuds to my knees, and I rock it to the side so I can see. The girls are whimpering and William just stands there looking at his old boots, hands balled in his pockets and digging at the seams. My mother is talking to two men beside her, their heads nodding fast as she gestures toward me. Wet wool sticks to my shoulders, my chest. The ground grinds against my tailbone. My hair strings wet streams over my crossed arms. The water drips in the dirt with a soft thump, and sinks down. My breath is loud in my ear pressed to my shoulder. Will no one come near me?

Suddenly, a hand against my back, under my armpit, and a woman I've never seen before leans down, her eyes dark and big, an inch from mine, yellow sleep crumbs stuck to the corners. She whispers, "You have heard, sister, we've known those words too," and helps me to my feet.

Jane Helped Me to My Feet

She gave me fresh milk and taught me how to sing.

She held my shaking limbs.

When I was to marry, she told me to love Abraham

as I would a brother, to touch

only as two innocent children might.

She sewed my wedding dress

of Turkey Red, and strew orange blossoms in my path.

She tied the horseshoe round my arm

and led me to the gate.

God will show you the way, she said. She opened the gate.

For years, I heard God's whispering,

but I did not walk in it. I followed

the paths of men

until they led me into briars.

I walked through the briars

and came out on the other side, scratched

and torn, my blood as red as anyone's.

In America, Anything Will Grow

1762, Manchester, England

Winter. Dead grass stalks covered with snow and soot. I lean in the doorway,
feel the tenderness under my breast, the curve into shadow. My hand
trembles. Abraham at the blacksmith shop with Papa. He was all smiles
when I told him. Huge hunger, that man. Always snaking under my skirts.
Well, no more of that now I'm in this way, I told him, and he blushed when I
slapped him away. Bed's cold these nights, low on coal. I won't be able to
work at the infirmary, after, and then where will we get the money? So cold,
I have to push close just to sleep and that gets him moving, even in his
dreams. Wind wings blowing in here, makes him mad when he gets home.
Better go outside, shut the door. Weeds between tight houses all mad. I'd
like a garden, come spring. Jane says I can have some seeds, see how they
come up. This soil isn't good for growing. Jane says that deeper in there
are fewer rocks, darker dirt. She says that in America, anything will grow;
it's got golden soil. And open spaces, too, where the clouds hunger. Clouds
cling here like burrs to the smoke. So cold now–the baby takes all the heat,
all the food, all the strength.

Beginnings

I birthed four, fragile as ice forming
     against the gutter's edge.
          The first's blue lips
               never broke through sound.

The next two
     caught whooping cough.
          I remember steam condensing
               on the blanket tent, damp on my shoulders,

spit tinny in my mouth.
     Lizzy shaking so hard
          I dropped her in the water basin,
               scalded my fingers pulling her out.

She couldn't breathe through
     the screams and coughing.
          Abraham tore the tent away.
            Cold air slapped my eyes.

Cold water through my arms
     over the quiet, steaming body.
          The last—Mary—made it to four.
            She had a mole that matched mine,

low on the hip bone,
     and a crooked eye that followed
          the other like a sigh.
            Abraham made her an iron girl

from shop scraps. I gave her wool squares for dresses.
She'd take the doll to bed
and I'd wake with the cold head
pushed into my neck.

After the Fourth Burial

1770, Manchester, England

I fell asleep out by the oak, and Abraham found me in the morning on his way to the shop. I had lain on an ant pile. They crawled over my legs, through my hair; one even worked up into my nose and I sneezed it out. Hard to breathe, thin mucus sliming my top lip. He wiped it with my wet sleeve and picked me up. I was so limp, helpless. The sky was clear that day and I thanked him for that blue after the rain, my lips moving like worms. Labor just to slit my eyes open. My heavy head rolled down into the crook of Abraham's arm and his chest, and the scent of wool mixed with mud filling me with joy but why? My cheek was melting into the rough sleeve, and the blood throb in my head echoed the flow through his arm. Through swollen eyes, I watched the neighbor children throw mud at each other—one tall, skinny girl without a shirt running after her young brother with mud-caked hair. Her breasts just beginning to bud. She caught him and smeared more mud in his hair, and he scratched her stomach. They stopped still when Abraham passed, whispering like leaves, the boy standing in front, a shield.

Bring Thy Gift to the Altar

"Follow me," the voice said.

> The scent of lilies, of crushed sweetgrass.
> Water burning on my tongue.

"Ye weep . . ."

> Fingers rubbing my bottom lip
> as I would touch one of my babes
> to make her open her mouth for food.

"Ye weep?" A question, soft as the first spring rains.

> I had nothing to hold the water.
> It seeped from cracks in the bowl of my body.

> The touch of warm oil upon my forehead.
> On the soles of my feet.
> The sweet-woody animal odor of spikenard.

"Let not your heart be troubled."

> My heart slowed.

Then the voice again: "Barley loaves." A laugh, a trickle in the throat.

> "Barley loaves?"
> Again, the laugh, fresh as uncut sage.

"Gather the fragments that remain, that nothing be lost."

A mountain by the sea,
five thousand in the crushed grass,
five loaves in a basket,
two hundred pennyworth of bread, two fish.
From the fragments enough
to fill twelve baskets.

"I will see you again."

❧ ❧ ❧ ❧ ❧ ❧ ❧ ❧ ❧ ❧ ❧ ❧ ❧ ❧ ❧ ❧ ❧ ❧ ❧ ❧

Cold pottage. Pickled oysters. Ten potatoes. Six shirts to scrub, two mouths at my breast, three lumps of lard soap left. Five sheets to string. Dough rising, two loaves on the peel, and sleep now sleep, no don't cry, that coughing batters your breath. A rub of camphor and honey, and more wood for the fire, water from the well. Blood pudding, frumenty and boiling bones. More wood for the fire, more water from the well. All the linens soaked through. Ten potatoes, six shirts to scrub—and dirty linens, dirty linens are never through—ashes, bread, urine—

❧ ❧ ❧ ❧ ❧ ❧ ❧ ❧ ❧ ❧ ❧ ❧ ❧ ❧ ❧ ❧ ❧ ❧ ❧ ❧

"Joy." A ewe, an olive grove.
"I will not leave you comfortless." Blue iris, hyacinth, an egg under the leaves.
"No more the anguish." A thing much whiter than an egg.
"Follow me." The young of a white goat so like a child after its mother.
"And your heart shall rejoice." With my two arms I do not aspire to touch the sky.
"Arise—let us go."

So great a sweetness flows into my breast;
I must laugh and I must sing.

Manchester Constables' Log

July 13, 1772

        daughter
        of the Peace

John Lees and Ann Lees,
appear before Justice
Peter Mainwaring

July 14, 1772

        the Shakers

5 Shillings and Sixpence:
To Ale for 24 Persons
About Apprehending

October 19, 1772

        making good
        the breaches

        lock't up there

5 Shillings, Two Pounds:
To repairs

at Lees in Toadlane
in order
to apprehend a gang
of Shakers

May 30, 1773

        in the Old
        Church

Ann Lees a Shaker
apprehended for disturbing
the Congregation

July 27, 1773

On Saturday last ended
the Quarter Sessions here,
when the following persons
were tried: John Townley,
John Jackson, Betty Lees, and

in the Time of Divine Service

Ann Lees (Shakers)
for going into Christ Church
in Manchester, and there
willfully and contemptuously
disturbing the congregation
then assembled at Morning
Prayer, were severally fined
Twenty Pounds each.

And Charles Gafkell,
charged with stealing a wallet,

acquitted.

The World's Course

Cures

Sold by Mary Berry and Sons in the Market Place and Thomas Berry in
Hanging-Bridge, Manchester. By the King's Royal Patent.

Dr. Lowther's Specific Powders and Drops, (for) every species of Fit, whether
Epileptic, Convulsive, Hysteric, Hypochondrial, or Paralytic. Twelve years'
experience with uncommon success, confirms their not only curing, but
being a most certain preservative against Apoplexies, are perfectly innocent,
and may be taken by either Sex, at all Times, and Infants. Priced at 3s each
Bottle and Packet.

Cloth

Exactly at 2 o'clock sold in Berry's Auction Room, several sorts of goods,
consisting of Ribbons, Gloves, Stockings, Waistcoat pieces, Gawz, Lawn,
Muslin, Broglios, Lasting, Grograms, Dresdens, Woolen Cloth, Nankeen,
Handkerchiefs, Calamancos, Jacks, Dowlas, Sheeting, Linen Cloth, Pictures,
Coverlids, Frize, Watches, Feather Beds, and other Goods.

Exactly at 4 o'clock will be sold 38 bundles of white 3 Crown Hambro Yarn,
368 lb of white Yarn, two casks of Fine American Ashes and 4 casks of
fine ditto Pot Ashes, and White Hambro Malt and Irish Yarn. Also part of
the Stock of Mr. Thomas Harthorn, Bankrupt, consisting of Weigh Beams,
Buttons, Weights, Coffee Mills, Bellows, Coal Boxes, Smoothing Irons, and
a painted sign 15 foot long. Also a complete one horse Chaise, with the

Harness. Also a very genteel Black-boy Mare, 5 years old, near 15 Hands high, got by Hector, and warranted sound.

Price of Corn, &c, Saturday July 13, 1771

Wheat, 320 lb. Wt. per load from 35s to 38s
Flour, 240 lb. ditto, from 34s to 37s
Oatmeal, 24 lb. ditto, from 28s to 32s
Oats, 9 Winchester Bushels, ditto, from 14s to 28s
Beans, 15 ditto, from 21s to 25s
Barley, 20 Pecks
Beef per pound 4d to 5d

To be Fought

at the New Cock Pit, in Preston,
A Match of Cocks, betwixt Edward Dicconson, & William Hulton, Esqrs.
To begin on Monday the 17th of this Instant June, and fight
the three following days.

The Ladies New and Polite Pocket Memorandum Book, for 1772

containing 532 leaves of superfine paper ruled in the most plain and useful manner for keeping an Account of Expenses throughout the year, and for setting down Appointments, Visits, Memorandums, and Observations, with every Day and Week in the year distinctly marked. Likewise the following useful and interesting particulars, among many others: The Triumph of the

Hymen, a humorous Tale. The New and esteemed Songs and Country Dances.
Select Poetical Pieces of Wit, Humour and genteel Gallantry. An essay on
Beauty, considered under the particulars of Color, Form, Expression, and
Grace. Valuable Receipts in Cookery, Pastry, and Confectionary. A familiar
introduction to the most entertaining Parts of Astronomy. Ironical Instructions
for becoming disagreeable in all Companies, and upon all occasions. Holidays.
The Changes of the Sun and Moon. Tables ready cast up for various Uses, &c.

Ran Away

from his master, Peter Ward, Hat-maker, in Manchester,
about the 30th of June 1772. Brown hair, had on when he went away
a green olive-drab Thickset Coat, and red cloth waistcoat, and Leather
breeches.

Ann Lord, 14 years, an apprentice, has a touch of the Evil on the right side
of her face, had on a blue Gown, with Clogs and Buckles to them.

Stolen

Black mare, small star on her forehead, wheel-fired in the round bone of the
rear side. Black mare, a white Blaze down her face, one white Heel behind.
5 Guineas reward offered by owner.

Stolen from the Parish Church. Two Communion Flagons, Two large Silver
Salvers, One large Silver Dish, Four Silver Chalices.

Tuesday September 8, 1772

A Letter from Dolgell, in Mirrineth Shine, North-wales, informs us that a
Methodist Teacher attempting lately to preach there on Market Day, the
inhabitants drove him out of town and threw him and his horse into a deep
pool, where they inhumanly set a great Dog at him, which seized the horse by
the nose and plunged him several times under the water, whilst they pelted
the Preacher with stones, but this not satisfying their Brutality, they sent for
more dogs to worry the poor man, but the Dogs mistaking their business, fell
to fighting with each other, by which the attention of the mob being drawn off
from the Preacher, he escaped with his life—

A Few Days Ago Died

in Padiham in this county, of a Cancer of her Throat, one Sarah Sharrock,
above 50 years of age, whose Tongue dropped out of her Mouth into her own
hand, about 12 days before she died.

In the course of last week were interred at Rochdale, two women, who died of
the abuse they had received from their husbands.

Bid Others Come to the Feast

1772, House of Correction, Manchester, England

Christ came with figs and wine and fruits,
    glossy skinned and golden.
        The table spread with silver and myrrh.
He opened his arms.
    His heart beat against my cheek,
        warm, *like leaven, hid in three measures*
            of meal, till the whole was leavened.

He was laughing.
    The scent of bread rising, baking.

        All things are visible
            if you choose to see.
                A flicker of light in the corner
                    of your eye–an angel.
      We use parables
           because there are no other ways
              to describe the truth.

        Our body a grain of sand.
          Our faith a mustard seed.
            Our love a marriage feast.
              An uncovering of sight
              to the blind.

The kingdom of heaven is—

Who will show you the way?

"This is my body," he said.
   The cracked skin of his fingers on my lips.
      "This is my blood," he said.

                  A woman at the mouth of a cave
                     singing. Lines in stone.
                        Inside her hands,
                           the stone took shape:
                              horse, lion, bird, man.
                  She set the white stone down.
                     It was stone again.
                        She took a bowl of water
                           and she drank.

                              ✸

My bones dark with cold,
   curled on the stone.
      Legs heavy as lead.
         Christ pulled me forward.
            "Do men gather grapes of thorns?" he asked.

A two-story house built of wood. The door was open.
   In the kitchen, three girls dried the last dishes, stacking bowls.
   They wiped their wet hands on their aprons.
         "Sister, sister," they called, a slow forming
            of words in the mouth, like light
               through the windows.

"They say you are Mother's buntling," one said to another.
The second blushed and laughed. A well-struck bell.
"She brought me in from the hedge;
I was a little brown bird."
The first girl lifted her hand to the other's
cheek, to feel the heat.
"Now you are a little red bird," she sang.
Wingtip to wingtip.

The third girl stacked the last bowl.
The earthenware rang.
Then she walked to the open doorway,
to the large room where many had gathered.
She clapped three times.
"Mother will be here soon!" she sang.

"I know these girls," I said to Christ.
"But where, where? That house—
the fruit?"

"They are your children—" he said.

I took hold of Christ's warm hand.
My body broke into light.

"What must I do?"

"Bid others come to the feast."

֍ ֍

James's voice was hoarse through the keyhole.
The women faded away.
Christ faded away.
It was dark.

A pipe scraped through the narrow hole.
Liquid dripped on the floor.
"Put your mouth on it," James whispered.
Milk and wine ran down my chin.

Sabbath Breaking

I spoke of
        God
                    in seventy-two
  languages
and still
     they would have nothing
but my body broken.
                Bound
with rope,
          knocked with clubs,
                   kicked
every two miles. They stoned me
                in the
  valley
as the sun set,
         emerald and citrine.

The stones beat
         like hot hearts
inside
     their clenched fists.
When they opened:
                  doves
thunder

A Found Handfast

Nine Shakers set sail in May 1774, from Liverpool for New York, aboard the Mariah, *under a Captain Smith.*

The storm met us halfway, wounded the hull.
Bottom plank pulled back like a bent finger,
vessel heavy with water tearing in.
Captain Smith screaming:
Buckets! Hands! God!
God gifts us with dance: the bright wings
of an angel watching in the sky above.
Our feet slip as the wet deck bucks.
Air grays even the closest faces
as the nine of us turn and turn.
Turning, Nancy falls forward; her chin hits wood.
Her hands hold the gash, blood running
ribbons over fingers, wrist, elbow.
Wiry waves wash her sprawled body
back toward the edge.
I crash forward, skirts wet to my waist,
arms spread as if to lift her.
The sinking ship pounces and I flounder,
knees screeching as they give—
Salt scalds my eyes and I am reaching blind
believing in a found handfast.
Then I feel her catch and hold,
longing for life tight like cable
binding lowered sails to the naked, shaking mast.
I am only a small woman, but God
sings strength through tendons, bones.

I lift us both to our feet.
And now we sing, swinging linked arms in prayer.
No gale or leaning will loosen our circle dance,
dissolve our joined notes.
Not even the Captain,
his red face blank with fear.
A wooden bucket smacks my back
as he swings in panicked circles, swearing
he'll throw us overboard if we don't bail.
I answer: not a hair on our heads
    shall be harmed.
We are singing sea and sky,
heaving our voices between wind and wave
while wounds raise sailors' wails.
I've done this before: eyes set straight,
heart beating wings, breath breaking open.
Sea pulses in me, pushes out of me.
I am ocean, world bones,
wounded and wounding, washed and washing.
I am Ann the Word, ground in God's glory.
A simple song is all it takes.
Everyone is shouting: *Lord, we perish!*
when a wave drives the plank back in place.
Worn, I sink to my knees.
My cold skirts cling.
Captain Smith stares hard.
His scabbed hand warms my forehead,
I don't know if you're a witch or . . .

We touch ground sixteen days later,
our legs unsteady on this new earth.

THE NEW WORLD

'Tis the gift to be simple, 'Tis the gift to be free,
'Tis the gift to come round where we ought to be.
And when we find ourselves in a place just right,
'Twill be in the valley of love and delight.
When true simplicity is gain'd,
To bow and to bend we shan't be ashamed.
To turn, turn will be our delight,
'Till in turning, turning, we come round right.
—"Simple Gifts"

The Human Press

1774, New York City

Fly Market thick with blood, human cries, and corn
from Long Island. Women with bright hats cluster
as butchers call their orders, and cleavers
chop red chunks from pig, cow,
the thud as steel bites wood and sticks.
Saturday and walking's a trick—find a way
to slip between crowds, bodice brushing jacket backs.
Stuck between taller bodies, a skyscape of turning heads,
one must learn to push lightly against threadbare sleeves.
A man pinches the blue wool skirt
of a woman in front of me, then disappears
in the thick human press toward the pier.
Another hold of slaves hunch like shadows
toward auction pens, reeking of urine and salt.
Dark fingers hook my skirt as a girl passes, red eyes like hellfire,
as tall as Mary when she died, hair matted with dried dung.
Her mother yanks her away, my skirt lifting as she's hefted toward a hip.
When I reach to touch, she flinches, lets go.

Children are born into soul slavery every day. There's no need
for carnal pleasing, for staining our flesh with breeding sin
like flies fondling each other on hanging carcasses.
Can they see? No children and the kingdom of God is at hand.
The world turns again. We are meant for more.
I am Ann the Word, but who here will have heard?
My baskets are heavy and I have a sick husband to feed.
Yet I believe, I believe.

There's a place I go to hear.
The marsh below the city cradles me
when human voices gnaw God's quiet talk
like muskrats at reed grass roots.
Rushes knock thin arms against the wind,
shivering as I sing wet ground up bared soles
and spine to pale sky. I am the willow
bending God's breath, sweet clover
palming the earth green.

A Palace When You Come

My hand in brother William's is blue tinged as he kneads it between his
own. Scour of calloused skin. His smithing scars stand out, two on his
left knuckles, an angry round eye on the meat of his thumb. The sleeve
of his gray jacket brushes his wrist as the chill spring wind buffets us. He
is heading north up the Hudson on a chokecherry sloop to find land for
us, for our heaven. He and James and John. His voice, so low I can hardly
catch it: "Good-bye now, dear sister, dear friend, dear mother." The captain
calls the all-aboard. Concern like a small rip as our bodies pull away. "You
will come? You will come when he is better? I will send for you if you do
not come soon." "I will come," my voice quiet, calm, a sweetness I hardly
remember, a dove call I heard a lifetime ago. "We will have it ready for you
when you come." His head bent over mine jerks up, and he smiles his quick
smile, gone before I know it was there. His hand rubs mine in excitement.
"A palace. We will have a palace for our kingdom, when you come."

Cherry blossoms float down from the trees into the dark water, rest for a
moment on the surface before they are lost in the sloop's wake.

Light Adds Flesh

Autumn 1775, New York City

Mornings, I start more wash—
    haul cold water from the square,
        light a fire, put the iron on the stove.

The stockings and gauze soak
    while I pound sheets for boiling.
        Abraham rasps, lying on his back.

The thick breath batters his lungs
    like hooves on cobbled roads.
        His right hand twists the sheets in sleep,

turning a corner into a horn or gourd.
    Sun comes closer, nudges his shoulder,
        the sweat-soaked cloth beneath.

How thin he is: a picked bone.
    Light adds flesh, warming neck and cheek.
        When it reaches his eyes, he'll wake and cough,

surprised at his own weakness.
    Sometimes I lie next to him,
        my head on his chest,

hearing his heart beat.
    Uneven. Footsteps walking away.
        I wonder why he didn't leave

when I rebuilt God's road
    over our marriage bed.
        The way to eternal spring.

Sparrow and wild rose.
    Frail as dry leaves, he
        could never pull me back.

Still, my heart jumps
    when he reaches
        into the space between.

The Greased Gander

Gray feathers slicked, he's small as a wool jacket wet and bunched. His head held up by thin birch sticks, horizontal, jammed tight to the neck. Clawed, knobbed feet close and open, hooking, unhooking air, and the beak the same, but for the wet, choking sound. A man on a horse trots by, reaches with his left hand and yanks from the feet, his torso twisting back as the horse keeps moving forward. His hands slip from its greased body, and he falls back on the saddle, then jerks forward, his nose hitting the horse's neck. Thick, snarled laughter from a group of mounted men down the street. One man claps and whistles. When I walk forward, he yells, *Outta the street, woman*, kicks his horse's flank. The black gelding jumps and skitters to the side, then bounces into a quick trot, iron shoes ringing stone. The bird's mangled squawk cracks the air and then the horse is past, the man swearing as he nudges it to a walk and stops near the man he laughed at. The gander's neck is rubbed raw and blood oozes out, beads on the oily feathers. I'm rooted to the side of the street, arms locked at the elbows, teeth grinding as I watch the bird heave. The jabber of tavern talk wafts from an open door behind me—men placing bets on the bird's death. Dropping my baskets, I rush toward the hanging gander, but already another horse hurtles toward it, blocking my path. In a flash, the brown body is gone, leaving a cloud of warm meat stench, and I am tottering on my toes, still trying to slow down, staring up at the gander's torn neck.

Spring's Coming

1776, New York City

Baskets heavy, rubbing wool raw at my inner elbow, filled with food—blue fish, winter squash, chicken, ground flour. Soiled clothes from the woman who sells potatoes fill the other basket. Rained this morning. Street stones shiny gray, bits of quartz sparking in the afternoon sun. Peaked row-house roofs dripping streams down corners. Twice a week I make this round. Six blocks down to the Fly Market near South Street, next to the ferry where we docked half a year ago or more. Late March now. Abraham sick all winter. Still weak, but growing tougher as the sun strengthens. He can walk to the window now and lean halfway out—nearly scares me to death, how he bends at the waist, arms spread as if he could take in the whole busy street: the red-brick, timber-framed row houses rubbing against each other, the Round Arm Inn, steep roofed, where men jib and smoke outside, mouths steaming out more cloud than their pipes some days, and the blacksmith crammed next door to the stable. Through the open door, the red glow of heated metal. Abraham had a job there till he grew sick with fever and his lungs thickened on breath. This morning, his face red and bright as a child's, he yelled *Good Morning* out the window. His smile wide as my open hand, to know he could make such a sound again. Men before the tavern stopped and waved, tipping their hats, and a woman walking quickly with her daughter, knee height, hand in hers, gave him a glare and sped up, nearly dragging the girl behind. Ben, the blacksmith, yelled back, his boot grinding grass just begun to grow between cobblestones: *Abe, sound like you'll be back at it again soon, aye?*

Abraham Left Me on a Thursday

They'll say he was a bad man, but I know how hard it is to live with God. *In the flesh, in the flesh, where are you Ann? You're a spirit banging at your own rib cage.* His face wrinkled, hair springing wild from behind his ears. A thick white-gray shock, a thumb's width, sprang above his forehead, falling to both sides. Still a tall man, but the illness stooped him. Even so, my head reached his collarbone. After the others went ahead, he got better. When I came back from seeing them off at the dock, he danced me across the room, laughing, the heat from his grip burning my side. I shook my head, *No, Abraham, no,* and he stumbled. We fell sideways to the floor, tangled, my cheekbone pressed to the wing of his shoulder, the rough weave of his hemp shirt. I could smell sweat soaking the cloth, strong with fear and sadness.

Mosquito Song in the Time of Poverty

1776, Niskeyuna, New York

Kwe Katsi.
She:kon, Mother Ann.
At times she came and sat along the bank
and shared some songs.
Mary, her Christian name.
She:kon a friendly greeting,
deer sudden in the trees.

I tore chunks of rye, still morning warm.
She taught me kaná:taro, bread.
In her hands, dried raspberries:
skenekwen: tará nen.

Wings droned around our ears.
She closed up. Sad mosquito
whispering his tale. Tahsakohroria:ne
ne tsi nih brother fighting o:ten.
He is poor. He has nothing for us.
Black hair shorn short in mourning.
Her first baby, bread to share,
died in her hands before the naming.
She told me in her fingers weaving
and unweaving baskets of torn grasses.
Milk still seeping from her breasts.
Her brother fighting with Brant for the British
would not cross water today.

Milk-clotted cloth. She rolled her eyes.
Okariata:ne always the same message.
She shook her head and wiped his wings away.
So old-fashioned, my spilling tears.
Ne se aonha:a across the bridge—
her corn flats, yellow in the leaves.

We sang it again:

Okariata:ne tahotharatie
Tahsakohroria:ne ne tsi niho:ten
Ne se aonha:a thorihwaka:ion thorihwaka:ion
Mosquito is bringing us a message:
He wants to tell us how poor he is.
He's so old fashioned and always
brings the same message.

The Smallest Injuries

I.

Our first winter Nancy's hands cracked
and bled. The blood crusted, then broke
when she bent her fingers around
the spoon to stir the soup or fold
the blanket on her bed. At night
we rubbed lard into skin. I warmed
it first over the fire; still, she winced
as I kneeled down, even before
my palm smoothed over her knuckles.

II.

James turned somersaults when spring came
his hair a halo in the sun,
pant legs slipping to his knees.
Hooting and hollering, arms smeared
with clover, mud, strawberry leaves.
The hum of birds and bees gone mad
drowned his shriek. Hopping up and down
he held one hand closed. *Oh James,*
let me pluck the sting.

III.

While cradling hay, William twisted
his ankle on uneven ground.
His scythe slipped and sliced through the boot.
Soaked with clotting blood, his sock clung
to threads of skin around the wound.

Laugh, William, laugh, I said, and poured
cold water from the well. *Or sing!*
My fingers brushed away the flies
to wrap the linen tight. He wept.

Make the Bridge the Truth That Is Coming

Autumn 1778, Niskeyuna, New York

Two years we'd waited for our time
to come, and William's question wrung
my mind that morning: *Will our truth*
ever open to the world, Sister?
They will come like doves, my brother.
I turned back to the song, clapping
quickly. *But they do not come yet,*
he said. I heard the brush of grass
as he walked down the hill. The others
grew silent, and the wind rushed in
and tore dry leaves from the oak.
Hannah tucked her hands underneath
her armpits; John bit his lip.
I knew winter was coming too.
Last year, the rats ate our grain.
William waited up those nights—
his gunshots cracked our sleep
and rat blood streaked our floorboards.

Go. My throat closed on bitter spit.
Be patient. They will come. They will.
I left to walk among the trees
that edge the stream, singing *God,*
I am a woman listening.
A kingfisher lit on a branch
and I stood still, watching his breath

rise and fall in his breast, my breath
rise and fall in my breast. I turned
to see more clearly, but he flew
upstream. A branch broke from the tree.
I sank to my knees. Late mosquitoes
stung me, then lurched blood drunk
and heavy on their wings.

He Comes and Asks to Plant

I felt the hidden stones, wet
in his soiled fist. How tight
he held them. Three seeds:
Ashmead's Kernel, Winesap, Pippin.
So still they were, waiting
for burial and new life.
He was still like that, this man.
Even as his hands broke
the earth he worked, his heart
was fallow, asleep.
I did not turn;
I waited for a sound,
for that shivering first movement.
Sun streamed over our damp land,
the heat steaming the marsh.
Still, the air tasted cold.
How long could he hold
those stones, hesitant, ungrown?
He planted his hands;
They grew fingered branches
thick with cherries, plums, and peaches.
He would bear true fruit:
apples whole, unfallen.
I turned and told him,
Yes. Plant. Plant everything
as if you had eternity,
for you will die tomorrow.

The New Light Revivalists Wait for Their Redeemer

1779, New Lebanon, New York

The Voice of the New Lights:

While the Rebels captured and recaptured Fort Ticonderoga
and the British raided farms up and down the Hudson Valley
from Canada to New York City, butchering six sows here,
five bulls there, feeding their horses with our saved grain,
or even taking our horses if theirs were slain, and, worse, stealing
our men at gunpoint to fight, or breaking our homes
with long battles, bullets in the walls, the windows shattered,
the food finished, the animals all slaughtered,
while Clinton burnt Kingston down to the ground,
and every farm in his path, and the fires
filled the skies with dark smoke so every breath
we took was acrid and bitter with fear and hope,
we prayed for an end.

Every night we were visited by visions of the millennium,
the end of story, fire and falling stone, our souls
at the gate. Even the stouthearted fell
like men wounded in battle, screaming and shouting
before the great light. We knew the redeemer
was coming on his bright chariot, his hands full
of roses and doves, healing all wounds with his blood.

Summer spilled into autumn. We harvested the corn,
the wheat, the root crops, though truly we believed

there was no need, for soon time would come to an end.
Then winter with her strong winds, her blank days,
muffled our hope; and we fell into the arms of despair,
for we had seen the light and now were empty.

Had we overlooked our Lord? Had we passed by
and not seen? Had Christ come like a thief in the night?
All we could do was be watchful, be patient and wait.

The First Conversions

April 1780, Niskeyuna, New York

They came that third spring, early
while we were still in the frenzy of turning
thawed earth over, breaking up the winter-
thickened clumps with a quick jab
of pitchfork, side-smack of the shovel.

Two young men. They said they were headed west
to seek their fortune, but I could see how
they trembled like seeds
in the dark, warming with the touch
of sun-soaked soil. What they sought
was much deeper and closer.

We put them to work clearing trees:
cropping branches, felling the trunk,
digging deep for the root.
When they rested, their necks glistened with sweat.
I brought them water and sang.
New leaves unfurled in the wind.

That's when they asked me
if I thought Christ would rise again, and when—
William, my strong brother, raised his dark eyebrows
and his mouth muscles rippled. I too
could not hold back the glad laughter
which rose like a spring in my throat and ran over.

They sprang to their feet, offended, and turned to leave,
and so I knew they were true for the asking,
would be ripe for the gathering.
My sons, you cannot leave yet
for you have not seen what you came to find.

Christ has come. A thief in the night
is a woman sowing seeds at the break of day.

Birth. Mother's Heart will Staunch the Blood.

She comes to us heavy with child.
Winter bruised, soldier used.

I touch her sweat-wet brow.
A girl-child herself—hips still slender, hands like bone china—

yet stretched tight with the life inside her.
Motherwort to calm her.

Drink, child, this tea will ease you.
Blue-rimmed bowl, scrap rags of linen, a clean sheet.

Again her pain is near, swift river under the skin. Night and no moon.
Feed the fire with wood. The unborn's heel kicks down under her ribs.

Sing through the hurt, child—your song a boat on the rough.
Sing, child of the china hands.

Your babe kicks down.
Dance through the ring of fire. Kick down.

Your babe a bud, sticky with the sap of life,
how quick she slips from you now—

The cord unwinds from inside
and already you forget the pain for the joy.

Open–her eyes, and open–her mouth at your breast;
and you meet, at last, skin to skin.

Already, the new day is come.
Winter shaker, will you stay?

Hezekiah Hammond Speaks

Spring 1781, Niskeyuna, New York

I would not be made to stay.
While the strong ones still sang,
I slipped out the back
and made for my horse and the long ride home.
In the small stable, I breathed deep
the clean scent of straw, filled my mind
with the things of this world:
harness and heavy saddle,
rawhide whip, my own horse's salty flanks
and the muscles that moved beneath.

I had been chased here by a dream
of apples rotting on the tree and my children
hungry and worm eaten to the core.
They molded into the soil
and fed the seeds which grew dry leaves
that chanted *shaker, shaker* when the wind blew,
like the children on the road here,
who ran out from their houses
to throw small stones
at the legs of my mare.
No, I would not stay though my wife hoped
it might be a better way
than our starving in the dark . . .
the winter rye flooded
and two oxen dead.

But look, now they've found me out.
The tall one they call Father William,
with his large voice like a draft horse
pulling the plow through frozen fields,
will try at me again, I suppose.
I will not listen.

I will not listen, I will not look.
I'll fix myself upon my riding whip:
the lash cracks the air, then strikes the dirt
so dust rises and snags light from the open door.
A shield of falling dust stars hides me
from the too-bright, burning face.

When the last star settles, my whip lies curled
around my feet like a live thing, breathing.
I move my hand back, but then it jerks
and curves, slithering in the dirt,
snaking out from my body to strike
at the legs of the woman who has come
and stands in the doorway, blocking the sun.
Put down that whip and listen, you idle old man!
I drop it. It remains lifeless on the ground.
She steps over it, and close to me, so close
I feel her black jacket brush my coat buttons.
Listen! she hisses.
Then the great humming begins, burning
my blood, my bones, burning me from me
till I am only a spark in the roaring flame,
a spark that flies and falls and dies
at the feet of this woman—

When at last silence settles in my cracks,
I croak in a rusted voice, *I wish you would go home
and tell my family how it is with me:
the hand of God is upon me and I cannot go.*

Eat

Take an egg from under a hen.
Feel it warm the palm of your hand.
Close your fingers around it,
                              take it into
your skin, all that warm weight and curve,
the smooth beige flecked with brown.
You can feel the raised freckles and the scent
of earth and hay, manure warming
the shafts of sun inside the dark barn
and the sound of your own quiet breath
and the shifting, the settling of the hens' heated bodies,
the scrape of their claws moving the straw.

Now hold the egg close to a candle
so the light comes through.
See the dappled pores,
the scarlet branchings, the shadowed eye
of a body, the spider pulse. Pulse.
In the nest of your wrist and throat.
In the ear of the dark heart and belly.
                              Pulse.
                                        And silence.
Slip the egg back beneath the hen's heat.
Feel her feathers,
her shifting and re-settling, your breath.
The tongue in your mouth.

If, when the light shines, there is no body,
bring the egg back to the house.

These are small things for young minds
and are of great importance to me.
Never throw away the least crumb
of that which is prepared for you to eat
because you do not love it.

JOURNEY OF THE WORD

Tell them that we are the people who turn the world upside down.
    —Mother Ann

William Lee Asks If They Are Willing

June 1781, Harvard, Massachusetts

If they were willing to let us in, they would.
I never came into a place we were not wanted.
I always asked, loud and wondering,
calling out if they were willing.

And so we came to the Square House
and when I called a woman replied
that she didn't know as she was.
When I called again, she let on that she supposed she'd have to be.

So we came in and they fed us with what they had.
I left her an apple ere we left:
a wondrous red one I'd picked passing an orchard.
I left it there for to remind her we were coming back.

When I asked her if she didn't love us
a little, she shook her head,
but I saw the spark in her eyes.
I saw how Abigail looked at that apple.

Say to This Mountain, Move

Let's sit down in the doorway, here,
on these steps. We can talk some more.
The hens are scratching in the leaves
for aphids, acorns. That red one's new.
Molly calls her Joan of Arc: she fights
so hard, the others leave her be.
See the purpled scabs where she's lost
feathers–the broken veins inside
her eye, pierced by a beak or claw.
She holds it closed because it weeps. . . .

Molly will show her a button,
a ball of hemp, a plum, then turn
and hide them in her apron.
Joan'll cock her head and look around–
then come close, stick her beak inside
Molly's pocket. She knows the gifts
still exist though she can't see them.

And what of you, my child? Surely,
you have more faith than a chicken.

Would'st Thou Be a Child of God?

1781, The Square House, Harvard, Massachusetts

See here the washbasin and stacked dishes, all cleaned of dinner? Newcomers,
and there is young sister Jemima, that one I held as she tried to leave, a soul
I'd known before, her fast-beating heart, so scared, yet ripe for the setting free.
She tried to leave, but I heard the rustle of her skirt in the grass, the closing
door. I went after, calling out that she must come and say good-bye, at least—

           Listen, child, you are far from me. You have a long way to go, and you are
unsure   you want to go that way. You need to know to speak. Feel it in
your bones, let it   open like a poem, like a rose, let it bloom, bloom,
girl, bloom. You have a dark way   a dark turning, a denial, an ax for growing.
Put down your ax. Take this string   and follow it inside yourself.

Her slow turning and that first eternal step, her shoe wet with dew, the
tracking back like a doe nearing the open hand. I was still, so still, barely
breathing, calling *come back, this is your home.*

          This is your home. Feel your heart here, that soft throbbing, open
window,   the breeze blowing out all doubt. We will clean you here,
in the home   of your heart. Come child, come. See, that unstained press,
the barn beams, the clean   stacked hay in the corner and yes—
in the depth of sunlight, a shaft of dust   stars in the dark cool
the golden light of lit hay against shadowed, weathered   walls.

Fine dark strands clung to her damp temples, and red circles burned high
on her cheeks. Her hands clutched each other, her eyes were downcast,
watching the movement of her feet, then glancing up suddenly, nearly in

despair, as if she couldn't comprehend her stepping. Yes, that young girl's eyes were islands of fear swimming inside a sea of love. And yet, she came.

It is wherever we go, the open hand raised to the amazement, the wonder.
Feel   your gift, girl, your open bones splitting into light. You are all
the women   who came before; many, many have moved their hand in the
same patterns,   raising   the spoon from bowl to mouth, raising
the whole bowl. Others have sat   like you, hunched then straight backed,
the head bowed forward. Your mother's eyes,   your aunts', your grandmothers'.
We are at your back, sitting on your shoulders, our hands   holding you up like wings.

Nearly to me, she stumbled in a small hole and her step faltered.

There is a depth here, a deep hole, a well, a draining. Into the trees,
the shadows,   the moon lost in tall branches. Take my hand, child, do not
be afraid. I will walk   with you the whole way. Feel now, this steady
pressure, the warmth of my pulse   in the nest of my wrist.

I have found you, child, and I will not let you go.

A New Heaven and a New Earth

Ashfield, Massachusetts

> *And let him that is athirst come.*
> *—Revelation, 22:17*

They kept coming, on foot, by horse,
in sleighs slipping on the frozen mud.
We could not fit them all inside
Asa Bacon's three crowded rooms
and built a hall to hold our labor.
Their bodies warmed the room with dance
so strong the floorboards shivered, shook,
and those whose turn it was to eat
had to hold their trenchers steady.
The table rocked. William's tears of joy
ran down inside his mouth and mixed
with cornbread, salted beef in stew,
the apple cake Abigail made
from the last handfuls of wheat flour
before the Slossons' four sacks more.

The sky burned that night John counted
sixty sleighs, six hundred people.
The heavens streaked and throbbed, woven
in vermilion and verdigris.
We stood beneath the veil drawn back,
our breath beading on pine needles,

so silent we could hear the blood
flutter inside our wrist bones.

A rustling. Children tugged my skirt
and I leaned down. Molly's youngest—
her buntling—fat lipped from falling
down three stairs yesterday, whispered
Is this good? and stretched out her tongue
to show me, again, it wasn't cut,
and I replied, *Yes, yes it's good,*

spilling into laughter, a spark
that caught inside six hundred throats,
a spring so fresh we laughed till dawn.

The Dance

Days grind by, we do not sleep,
crying glory, grace, quench this thirst
folding unfolding joining spreading.
So heavy, the body: stone and root,
stone from the rotted fruit
dissolving back into the ground.
Ashes ashes, we all fall down.

My life, my life, I lay it down.

Blood moon. Scythes cradle the wheat.
In the temple, doves thunder. Rain.
We lift trembling fingers and touch
the edges of feathers. Their breath,
a wind of eyes within, winnows us,
our chaff rising like wings from seed.

The sound of many waters.
Shaken in a mighty wind.

Sloughed clean as a newborn calf
sticky with mother's blood. We burn
like sweetgrass, cedar, sage; with sap
and sweat, we weave the stalk: spine,
sacrum, and vein a psalm, open-
palmed dew on cordgrass, aster,
everlasting, bow down, bow down.

And the Spirit and the bride say, Come.

Again in our skin, our linen
chafes and burns. We are so tender.

Sister Jemima Watches Father William

I was too bashful to come near.
He stood at the pump, others in line behind.
A young brother by the name of John worked the handle,
pumping water in gushes for the others to wash.
Father William said something to him,
and he smiled wide and put one hand to his heart.
I could not hear over the sound of water
splashing onto the stone below.
Then Father made a cup of his palms.
The spring filled them and ran over.
Sun lit on the water; it became corded gold,
a living thing, a looking glass of heaven.

Learn to Sing by Singing

Oh, loved, beloved, you are dew on the jewelweed,
sheep among the lilies. The apple branch. The rapture
of bats and stars and grass singing, warm as new wine.

You are

the loved, my beloved–light in the bone, tender green,
the dinner bell ringing; aprons on the line–yellow muslin
and green–you are the end of the world and the first unfurling.

You are

the love, lemon and rind. Soft pine, cicada, swamp and vine.
Cattails at the edge of the road. Blue-eyed dragonfly.
Moon. Friend. Lizard in the woodpile. Sweet surprise.

You are the sky between my arms–

Blacksmith's Prayer, William Lee

Truth told, I got tired of meeting after meeting
and all the faces turning toward me
as if I had the answers.
Treat me no better than your brother.
Treat me as you would any brethren, brother,
I told them.
Still the sisters set aside butter for my potatoes,
and I would find small gifts beside my bed:
new socks, ripe cherries, a pair of fine boots,
my own holed pair taken away.

And every night, the heavy press of bodies
at meeting, the desperate surging of flesh and voice
to meet God. It is the way we knew
to bring them to relief, belief, to shake and sing
away the world, dance into the humble kingdom.
But sometimes I wanted to be alone,
feel the unrift heart of the blacksmith's fire,
know the ways metal melted and cooled,
so different from the human heart.
So who's to blame me
if at times I slipped away, felt again the heat on my face,
beat the metal into shapes? There, my soul
turned horseshoe, spoon, candlestick.
There, my sweat was prayer
as much as any song.

Black Guards

Winter 1781, Petersham, Massachusetts

First, they let us into the house.
My eyes dimmed
in the dark room.
Then rough hands burnt my ankles,
my back struck wood.
I was dragged like a carcass
through the snow.
Hefted and thrown into a sleigh.
No words could stop these beasts.
One man: tangled red hair,
mustache twisted like a snake,
pimpled cheeks, an eye marked
red by burst blood lines.
I whispered from my swollen mouth,
Even you, my friend, can be forgiven.
My jawbone bloomed with pain.
Heavy hand on my thigh;
another held my head back.
The horses breathed hard.
A rut or rock jarred the sleigh
and I flew forward, rolling under their feet.
A boot bruised my back.
Someone pulled me belly down over his knees,
slapped me as if I were a child.
Laughter like lines of hate,
like the sleigh runners knifing snow,
like the knife slicing the flour sack.

My mouth pushed against
another's pants. Stink of heat, moldy hay.
If God is a woman,
this is what she should be doing!
and dead eggs. I was emptied,
the sack of my body left on the road.

It Is Not I Who Speaks

And can he who smiles on all
Hear the wren with sorrows small,
Hear the small bird's grief and care
Hear the woes that infants bear—
            —William Blake

I have been walking with Christ in the groves and the valleys
and we have been speaking face to face.
Look, he says, and I touch the tissue-thin throat
with my little finger, and the sparrow shivers.
No bigger than a spool of thread,
the feathers not yet fully grown
and mottled blue the web of veins
inside the sticky lids, still shut.
Two ants crawl along the broken, folded wing.
The heart that shudders inside its breast
is warm, and the gurgled breath a song.
What would you have me do?

The Vessel, The Basin, Cold Earthenware

Devoured: the well, the stream, the bread and wine,
mantle of skin and fine-twined linen,
distaff and spindle creaking,
the cedar shuttle worn smooth
in the woof and weave, the loom.
Bitter the sting of lye-soak and dye,
the purple of violet darkened deep
stained poisonous blue, cut
with flint, hammer and chisel.
The wheel turns incessantly:
cruel root, alabaster stone.
Who has not lied, stolen, fought?

Withered up: the artery, the pulse
Double knotted in sackcloth of hair,
starved in the streets, the tongue shuddering,
a scanty pittance of bread, the flail,
a veil of goat's hair and scabs and scarlet threads,
stalks of flax spread to dry in the howling
wilderness: blind and weeping violet.
Is not the wound of the sword sweet!
And the broken bone delightful?
The girding knife drunk with blood.
No more dew nor rain: no more the spring.
The spindle turns furious
and the potter breaks the potsherds. . . .

Stretch out your hand
and I will take away the remembrance.
I will weave you a vessel
pure as snow, as milk.

Threading the Eye

This morning, James took in two lambs
from Krieger up past Pine Bush Road,
pastured them where thistles grow
among our flax, now blue in bloom.
We did not see them all afternoon.

William went to bring them in
and came back hunched, half-running,
cradling one, guts cupped in his hands.
He lay her on our long table;
breath, though light, still wet her nose.

Lucy! I called. She left her web
and loom to fetch hot water, rags.
We worked in silence, washing dirt
and dead bees from the sticky strands
before we tucked them back inside.

My hand trembled, threading the eye
as Lucy held the torn skin closed.
I winced at each stitch, pulling
the linen tight to seal her wound.
The lamb puked white mucus, then mewled.
Later, she sucked and walked a bit.

July Twentieth, Seventeen Hundred and Eighty-Four

Niskeyuna, New York

William watched the sunken head of his horse at the trough. He held on to the ash fence pole. His feet were bare and his toes dug into the dry dirt around the pole. He coughed weakly into his hand, and when he opened it, it was smattered with spit and blood. He took a handkerchief from his pocket and wiped his hand off. Then he coughed again, harder and for a long time, holding the cloth to his mouth. When he was done, he unfolded the cloth and lay it on the top of the fence pole.

The setting sun reddened the horizon. Ann came out of the house. Her dress was wet in front with the dishwashing. She held her hands out—they were softened and withered. The birds had grown quiet in the darkening of the summer night. The sun sank beyond the dark woods in the west and violet grayed the air. Between the sister and brother, the distance seemed suddenly infinite. The air resonated with waiting, as if each leaf trembled and then was still.

Ann entered the silence, moving across the yard without a sound until she reached William where he held onto the pole. He took his hand off the top of it, where he held the handkerchief, and pulled her in close to him. A small wind came up from the south, took the stained cloth and carried it over the fence. It landed for a moment on the ground next to the water trough. The horse lifted its head and looked at the scrap of cloth. Then, the wind came again, lifted it back up, and drew it across the pasture until they couldn't see it in the darkening light. From across the yard, a rooster cried, almost piteously, unsure, the sound fading out.

Inside the house, someone lit the lamps. Laughter spilled from the open doorways, from the propped-up panes. Moths pushed their bodies against the screens. Two men came out from the barn, stamping their work boots to free them of hay and dirt, and walked toward the house. A woman's voice began a song, and it was taken up by other voices. The men took off their boots and set them in order by the back door. They sang, too, as they unlatched the screen door and went inside.

"We've done good work," William said.

Ann said nothing. She held his hand very tightly.

William began to cough again, this time so hard his whole body bent over and he had to hook his arm around the pole to steady himself. He sprayed blood and spit over the ground in front of him, onto his own bare feet. When he finally stopped coughing, he gulped air.

Ann unpinned her handkerchief from her blouse. It was damp. She dropped heavily to her knees and wiped off William's feet. Her body was tired, too, and when she tried to stand, she found she couldn't. She stayed on the ground, holding the cloth, and wept. Her tears wet William's feet and she wiped them off. He put his hand on her head.

"Sister," he said. The rooster crowed again, stronger this time, its cry breaking the night.

"We've done good work," William said.

"Yes," she said.

William began to hum. Then he bent down, still humming, his one arm hooked around the pole, and got Ann's arm with the other one. Between the two of them and using the pole, they managed to stand again.

William stopped his humming. "Remember, Ann, when we were just young and went out to chase sheep?" he said.

Ann nodded.

"You'd run to one side of the field and I to the other, and we'd gather them up between us," William said.

Ann held the damp handkerchief.

"Remember, Ann?" William asked, almost pleadingly.

"Yes," she said. "You—jumping up and down in the air, all the way across, so far away."

From inside the house, the singing stopped. The crickets wound up in the silence.

"It won't be long, sister," William said.

One lamp went off in the house, then another window went dark. A murmur of voices as the rest were extinguished.

"No, it won't," Ann said.

They sang together. William's horse came close to the fence and he lay his hand on its forehead. Then the horse went away. Richard opened the pantry door and came out and listened to them sing. They sang until the coughing started. Then Richard walked across the yard and helped Ann lead William back to the house. They lay him in his bed, and Ann sat beside him all night. The next day, they sent six men with shovels to the small open field south of the apple orchard.

Mother Ann Tells Lucy What Gave Her Joy

A moment of understanding
    when the face lights up
        and even the trees seem to kneel.
The mossy ground
    below a huge willow
        by the side of the marsh.
Children who come
    with white faces
        and turn pink
            in the sun.

The sound of sawing in the woods
    and the long lone hum
        of a boat bearing lumber
            down the Hudson.
The sudden deer in the trees,
    a streak of white tail
        and the hoof prints
            filling with water.

The sound of voices
    rounding out with grace,
        with trust.
            And rosehip tea steaming in the sun.
How many times we threw off our shoes
    and danced together,
        the cool ground under our soles.
            And the mud! churned by feet, and horses,
        ox-carts and cows.

The open throats
    and closed eyes,
        that red ringing
            inside my heart.

And mornings that Lucy sang
    making breakfast,
        snatches of hymns
            stuck together.

The long, quiet time of waiting.

God Is the Mother of All

There is no end, there is no death.
Only the other breast.
My body, a song—
sing it, and it is gone.

The passing of the body is hard labor.
Pain and small surfeit of pain.

To be held in God's arms; to hear
the trumpets of her voice, a voice
I have heard faintly all my life,
as a babe inside the womb.

On September Eighth

1784, Niskeyuna, New York

Beside her brother's grave,
five men dig
a hole for Mother Ann
at the break of day.

A long procession
bears her body
through the rain.
James sings and weeps
weeps and sings
and weeps, singing.

The apples drip with rain.

Behold I Stand at the Door and Knock

Bring me your empty fields, roots
rotting in cellars, meager winter grain,
your candles, cradles, husks,
your sackcloth and swaddled dolls.

Bring me your lanterns, lightings,
your beds of chaff and flock, crocks of jam
and salted pork, your caddis, your holland
and huckaback, duroy and yellow nankeen,
your hatchel, hackle, heckle and flax,
your warm loaves on the peel,
tallow and raw hemp, jute tow,
your pipkins steaming with stew,
porringer and trenchers, your kneading trough,
pearlash for rising the sticky dough, your flagons
overflowing with small beer, cornmeal mush and molasses,
your pound cakes, gingerbread, nutmeg and cheese,
mint and anise and cumin
and currants dried before the flame,
johnny cakes and boiled potatoes,
coarse salt and honey,
chicken steamed with cider, tender beef,
the bone, boneset and bee balm, sassafras
and milk vetch, goldenrod and elderberry,
oswego tea, rosehips, winged sumac,
cold potting, brine, wicks and witching sticks,
your bellows and basins and awls, wimble
and gimlet, maul and auger, your reamer, your ripple

for broom corn, your iron coulter, leather crupper,
saddle stinking of sweat and wet straw,
your cards' iron teeth thick with pulling wool,
hogsheads of apples and pipes of grain, a tearce
of cider, a tearce of ale, your stilliard beam—
iron weight and scale,
cordage, flails and harrows,
your riddle a sieve for ashes and coals.

Search the lines in your hands,
the dark throbbing in your heart.
Your young children have fainted,
hunger at the head of every street.

Behold I stand at the door and knock:
seedlip and sweet apple in my hand.

Notes

I have drawn on the following print sources for my research:

Andrews, Edward Deming. *The People Called Shakers: A Search for the Perfect Society*. New York: Dover Publications, 1963.

Bishop, Rufus and Seth Youngs Wells, comps. *Testimonies of the Life, Character, Revelations and Doctrines of Mother Ann Lee, and the Elders with Her*. Hancock: J. Tallcott & J, Deming, 1816.

Brother Theodore E. Johnson. *Life in the Christ Spirit: Observations on Shaker Theology*. Sabbathday Lake: United Society, 1969.

Darrow, David, John Meacham, and Benjamin S. Youngs, *The Testimony of Christ's Second Appearing, Containing a General Statement of All Things Pertaining to the Faith and Practice of the Church of God in This Latter Day*. Albany: E. & E. Halford, 1810.

Evans, Frederick W. *Shaker's Compendium of the Origins, Principles, Rules and Regulations, Government and Doctrines of the United Society of Believers in Christ's Second Appearance*. New Lebanon: Auchampaugh Brothers, 1859.

Francis, Richard. *Ann the Word: The Story of Ann Lee, Female Messiah, Mother of the Shakers, the Woman Clothed With the Sun*. New York: Arcade Publishing, 2000.

Garrett, Clarke. *Origins of the Shakers*. London: The John Hopkins University Press, 1998.

Wells, Seth Y. *Testimonies Concerning the Character and Ministry of Mother Ann Lee and the First Witnesses of the Gospel of Christ's Second Appearing; Given by Some of the Aged Brethren and Sisters of the United Society, including a few sketches of their own religious experience: approved by the Church*. Albany: Packard & Van Benthuysen, 1827.

"I was once as you are; I had feet, but they walked in forbidden paths; I had hands, but they handled unclean things; I had eyes, but they saw nothing of

God aright. But now my eyes see, my ears hear, and my hands handle the word of life." Evans, chapter XI. 77.

Inside My Skin
Ann Lee was baptized in a private baptism at the age of six at Christ Church in Manchester, England. Francis, 8.

See D.A. Powell's biblically inspired work in *Cocktails* (St. Paul: Graywolf Press, 2004).

Early Work
"Winding the warps" describes how the vertical warp threads are measured and aligned on the looms, a job which the young Ann Lee likely did in pre-industrial England. Bishop and Wells, 3. See also Evans, 11. 2.

Mother's Touch
According to Shaker lore, Ann was averse to marriage from an early age. Darrow, 3.

Jane Helped Me to My Feet
Jane and John Wardley were tailors from Bolton, England who formed the Wardley Society (the first group of Shakers) eleven years before Ann Lee joined them in 1758 when she was twenty-three. By 1770, after undergoing years of spiritual tribulation, she received the revelation of the in-dwelling presence of the sacred. Ann was married to Abraham Standerin/Standley/Stanley in 1762. Francis, *Ann the Word*. 35–36.

Beginnings
Ann lost all four of her children while they were in infancy and early childhood. I have taken the liberty of naming her last child Mary. Andrews, 5–7. See also Francis, 37.

Bring Thy Gift to the Altar
The title is taken from Matt. 5:23 (AV). The final section is composed of Jesus's words as found in the Gospels, followed by reworked Sappho fragments.

Manchester Constables' Log
Gathered from *The Manchester Mercury* newspaper, July 27, 1773, as well as the *Manchester Constable's Accounts (1743–76)*, Volume III, ed. J.P. Earwacker, (Manchester: J. E. Cornish, 1892).

The World's Course
Gathered from ads in Manchester's newspaper, *The Manchester Mercury*, 1771–1773 (Microfilm, Sabbathday Lake Shaker's Collection).

Bid Others Come to the Feast
According to Shaker tradition, Ann Lee was imprisoned without food or water for two weeks in a cell so small she could not "straighten" herself out. While there, she was fed milk and wine through the stem of a clay pipe inserted in the key hole by James Whittaker, a young Shaker. Bishop, 50–53.

The woman at the mouth of the cave carving figures in stone is in response to the thirty-thousand-year-old artifacts found in Hohle Fels Cave in southwestern Germany in 2003. Marsha Walton, "Cave Art from 30,000 Years Ago?" CNN, http://www.cnn.com (December 18, 2003).

Sabbath Breaking
Shaker tradition records Ann's stories of religious persecution while in England. Evans, XI. 31–42.

A Found Handfast
The Shakers set sail on May 19, 1774 from Liverpool, England, and arrived in New York City on August 6, 1774. Francis, 81–83. See also Bishop 67–8.

"Simple Gifts"
A Shaker dance tune which was written in 1848 by Elder Joseph Brackett at the Alfred, Maine community. It was also used by Aaron Copland as a theme for variations in his *Appalachian Spring*.

Light Adds Flesh
While in New York City, Ann's husband Abraham became extremely ill; after he recovered, he left the Shakers for the world. See Bishop, 8, and Francis, 90–92.

Mosquito Song in the Time of Poverty
Contains broken bits of Mohawk language, as well as a translated song. In northern New York, the Shakers were neighbors with the Mohawk (Kanien'kehaka) tribe. There is mention in the *Testimonies* that William communicated with the Mohawk people in their language, and further mention of Native Americans showing Ann Lee reverence. Bishop 179, 201. Laura Redish and Orrin Lewis, "Mohawk Indian Language (Kanien'kehaka)," *Native Languages of the Americas*, native-languages.org. "Mosquito Song" and language found at Kanienkehaka Language Homepage.

Make the Bridge the Truth that Is Coming
Bishop, 12–14.

He Comes and Asks to Plant
Evans, chapter XI. 76.

The New Light Revivalists Wait for Their Redeemer
In 1779, a revival known as the New Light Stir broke out in response to the pending revolution and the millennial anticipation that had grown out of the Great Awakening. Garrett, 164.

The First Conversions
The nearby New Lights soon came into contact with the Shakers. This

poem draws on tree imagery attributed to Ann Lee on how to give a true confession. Bishop, 38. Wells, 39–41, 106.

Birth. Mother's Heart will Staunch the Blood
Winter Shakers were people who lived with the Shakers during the winter in order to survive, then left in the Spring.

Hezekiah Hammond Speaks
Bishop, 27–8.

Eat
The last stanza is from Mother's Work (roughly 1837–1860), a period of spiritual revival when individuals in the Shaker communities believed they had been visited by Mother Ann and given "gifts" of her wisdom in the form of teachings, drawings, and songs.

Epigraph for The Journey of the Word section: "Tell them we are the people . . ." Bishop, 318.

William Lee Asks If They Are Willing
Mother Ann and company traveled for two years and three months, visiting and strengthening communities in New York, New Hampshire, and Massachusetts. The Square House was built by a Perfectionist cult led by Shadrack Ireland, who died in 1780, a year before the Shakers arrived in Harvard. Francis, 164–173. Ann Lee had seen the Square House in a vision while in England (this vision is re-created in *Bid Others Come to the Feast*).

Say to This Mountain, Move
See Matthew, 17:20. Chicks as young as two days old possess the complicated skill known as object permanence. Regolin, et. al., "Delayed Search for a Concealed Imprinted Object in the Domestic Chick," *Animal Cognition* 1 (1998): 17–24.

Would'st Thou Be a Child of God?
Inspired by the conversion story of Jemima Blanchard. Blanchard, "Testimony," record., Roxalana Grosvenor (Western Reserve Historical Society Shaker Collection), VI: B-9.

A New Heaven and a New Earth
Ashfield, Massachusetts became a refuge for the persecuted Shakers. For more about this meeting and the vivid Northern Lights, see Bishop, 228. Also see Francis, 256–257.

The Dance
The Shakers conceptualized the Last Judgment as an internal process: "all the events described in *that book* [Revelation] would be accomplished in them as individuals." Evans, chapter IV. This poem conceptualizes the internal experience of Shaker dance worship by drawing on imagery and language from Revelation (AV).

Sister Jemima Watches Father William
For more biographical information about William Lee, see Evans, chapter XII.

Black Guards
Bishop, 91–8. Also, Francis, 205–210.

It Is Not I Who Speaks
Epigraph from William Blake's "On Another's Sorrow".
Mother Ann: "It is not I that speaks; it is Christ who dwells in me. . . If I walk in groves and valleys, there He is with me and I converse with Him as one friend converses with another, face to face." Brother Johnson, 7.

The Vessel, The Basin, Cold Earthenware
Influenced by language in the Old Testament (AV) and William Blake's "Jerusalem".

Threading the Eye
Lucy Wright became a future leader of the Shakers, helping to bring the disorganized believers into order after the death of Mother Ann, Father William, and Father James. She led the Shakers for more than thirty years. Garrett, 223.

God Is the Mother of All
See Brother Johnson, 6.

Behold I Stand at the Door and Knock
Many objects using colonial names are listed and include the following: chaff: grain husks: flock: refuse of wool or cotton, consisting of coarse tufts; cadis, holland, huckaback, duroy and nankeen: types of fabric; hatchel, hackle, heckle: combs with long metal teeth for cleansing raw flax or hemp; peel: tool resembling a long-handled spade, used to take loaves out of the oven; tallow: a mixture of animal fat refined for use in candles; jute tow: a course fiber from jute; pipkins: a small cooking pot or earthenware; porringer: a small dish for porridge, broth or other similar foods, usually having one handle; trencher: a wooden plate used at the table; pearlash: was used before baking soda to make bread rise; wimble and gimlet, auger: boring tools to make holes in wood; maul: a large hammer or mallet; reamer: a finishing tool with rotating cutting edge for enlarging or tapering a hole; ripple: comb for cleaning flax or broom corn; iron coulter: the iron blade fixed in front of the share in a plough which cuts the soil vertically; cards: toothed instruments used in cleansing wool by hand; hogsheads, pipes, a tearce: measurements in casks or barrels; stilliard beam: A balance for weighing that consists of a beam, a weight sliding on a graduated scale, and hooks to hold the thing being weighed; cordage: rope; flail: tool for threshing used to separate the grain or seed from the plant stalk; harrow: agricultural implement with teeth drawn over plowed land to break clods of earth; riddle: a coarse sieve used for separating chaff from corn, sand from gravel, ashes from cinders; and most importantly, the seedlip: a basket in which seed is carried in the process of sowing by hand. "Glossary of Colonial Terms," *History Online*, Chadds Ford Historical Society.

Acknowledgments

I want to express my deep-felt gratitude toward the following persons, without whom this book would not have entered the world: Jonis Agee for her unswerving encouragement and support, my editor Jim Cihlar for his perceptive insights, Ted Kooser and Hilda Raz for their ears and enthusiasm, my sister Lanya Ross for her constant companionship, my father and mother and kim-mother for their love and generosity, and my husband for his faith in me.

I also want to thank Brother Arnold and the Sabbathday Lake Shaker Community for the use of their library, as well as the humbling experience of partaking in a simple meeting.

"Learning to Sing by Singing" previously appeared on linebreak.org.

About the Author

Arra Lynn Ross grew up on a communal farm in Southwest Minnesota and attended Macalester College in Saint Paul, where she earned her BA in English. Her work has appeared in *Spoon River Poetry Review*, *Hayden's Ferry*, *Linebreak* and *Alimentum: A Journal of Food*. She is a PhD candidate at the University of Nebraska-Lincoln.

Founded as a nonprofit organization in 1980, Milkweed Editions is an independent publisher. Our mission is to identify, nurture and publish transformative literature, and build an engaged community around it.

milkweed.org

Milkweed Editions, a nonprofit publisher, gratefully acknowledges sustaining support from Emilie and Henry Buchwald; the Patrick and Aimee Butler Foundation; the Dougherty Family Foundation; the Ecolab Foundation; the General Mills Foundation; John and Joanne Gordon; William and Jeanne Grandy; the Jerome Foundation; Robert and Stephanie Karon; the Lerner Foundation; Sally Macut; Sanders and Tasha Marvin; the McKnight Foundation; Mid-Continent Engineering; the Minnesota State Arts Board, through an appropriation by the Minnesota State Legislature, a grant from the Wells Fargo Foundation Minnesota, and a grant from the National Endowment for the Arts; Kelly Morrison and John Willoughby; the National Endowment for the Arts, and the American Reinvestment and Recovery Act; the Navarre Corporation; Ann and Doug Ness; Jörg and Angie Pierach; the RBC Foundation USA; Ellen Sturgis; the Target Foundation; the James R. Thorpe Foundation; the Travelers Foundation; Moira and John Turner; and Edward and Jenny Wahl.

MINNESOTA
STATE ARTS BOARD

NATIONAL
ENDOWMENT
FOR THE ARTS
A great nation
deserves great art.

TARGET.

THE MᶜKNIGHT FOUNDATION

Interior design by Connie Kuhnz, Bookmobile
Typeset in Trajanus by BookMobile Design and Publishing Services

CPSIA information can be obtained
at www.ICGtesting.com
Printed in the USA
JSHW021822090922
30093JS00001B/1